from SEA TO SHINING SEA

MARYLAND

By Dennis Brindell Fradin

CONSULTANTS

George H. Callcott, Ph.D., Professor of History, University of Maryland, College Park

Robert L. Hillerich, Ph.D., Professor Emeritus, Bowling Green State University; Consultant, Pinellas County Schools, Florida

CHILDRENS PRESS®
CHICAGO

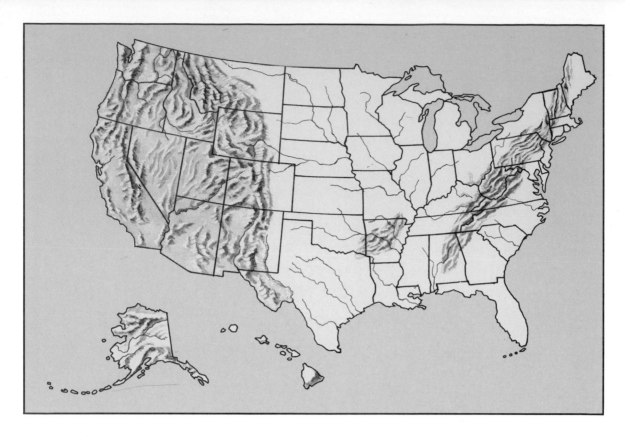

Maryland is one of the fourteen states in the region called the South. The other southern states are Alabama, Arkansas, Delaware, Florida, Georgia, Kentucky, Louisiana, Mississippi, North Carolina, South Carolina, Tennessee, Virginia, and West Virginia.

For my Aunt Florence Brindell

Front cover picture: State House, Annapolis; page 1: Sunset on Kent Island, Chesapeake Bay; back cover: Susquehanna River, Havre de Grace

Project Editor: Joan Downing
Design Director: Karen Kohn
Typesetting: Graphic Connections, Inc.
Engraving: Liberty Photoengraving

Library of Congress Cataloging-in-Publication Data

Fradin, Dennis B.
  Maryland / by Dennis Brindell Fradin.
    p.   cm. — (From sea to shining sea)
  Includes index.
  ISBN 0-516-03820-6
  1. Maryland—Juvenile literature. I. Title. II. Series:
Fradin, Dennis B. From sea to shining sea.
F181.3.F69   1994   94-6551
975.2—dc20   CIP
                                                          AC

Table of Contents

Chrysanthemums being grown near Greensboro

Introducing the Old Line State

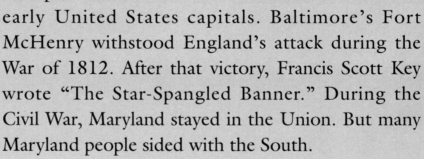

Only eight states are smaller than Maryland.

Maryland is one of the smallest of the southern states. But it has a long history. Maryland was one of the thirteen colonies. During the Revolutionary War, George Washington praised Maryland's "troops of the line." From that, Maryland took its nickname— the "Old Line State."

Baltimore and Annapolis served as early United States capitals. Baltimore's Fort McHenry withstood England's attack during the War of 1812. After that victory, Francis Scott Key wrote "The Star-Spangled Banner." During the Civil War, Maryland stayed in the Union. But many Maryland people sided with the South.

Today, many United States government offices are headquartered in Maryland. The state is well known for crabs, clams, and oysters. Maryland ranks high at growing tomatoes and raising chickens. Electrical machinery is made there.

The Old Line State is special in other ways. What state provided the land for Washington, D.C.? Where is the United States Naval Academy? Where were Harriet Tubman and Babe Ruth born? What state has a team named for its state bird? The answer to these questions is: Maryland!

Overleaf: Great Falls on the Potomac River

DUNNINGTON

MILK

A picture map of Maryland

Eastern Shore, Western Shore

EASTERN SHORE, WESTERN SHORE

Maryland is in the part of the United States called the South. Marylanders, however, think of their state as a Middle State—on the Atlantic Ocean, halfway between Maine and Florida. Pennsylvania bounds Maryland on the north. Virginia, West Virginia, and Washington, D.C., lie to the south and west. The Potomac River forms Maryland's southern and southwestern borders. Delaware and the Atlantic Ocean are to the east.

LAND AND WATERWAYS

Tundra swans and a Canada goose on the Choptank River

Maryland covers 10,460 square miles of land. Over 1,700 square miles of the Chesapeake Bay lie within Maryland. The Chesapeake Bay divides the state into two parts. Marylanders call them the Eastern Shore and the Western Shore. Maryland's Eastern Shore is a smooth lowland. The Pocomoke Swamp is there. Eastern Shore rivers include the Pocomoke, Choptank, Wicomico, and Nanticoke.

The Western Shore makes up the rest of the state. Maryland's largest city, Baltimore, is on the

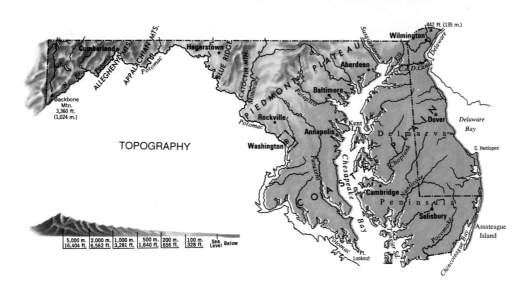

TOPOGRAPHY

Backbone
Mtn.
3,360 ft.
(1,024 m.)

| 5,000 m. 16,404 ft. | 2,000 m. 6,562 ft. | 1,000 m. 3,281 ft. | 500 m. 1,640 ft. | 200 m. 656 ft. | 100 m. 328 ft. | Sea Level | Below |

Western Shore. So is the state capital, Annapolis. Both cities lie on Chesapeake Bay. Just west of the bay, the land rises only a little above sea level. Next comes the Piedmont. This is higher, hillier land. The Appalachian Mountains loom over the state's westernmost two-fifths. Far-western Maryland has the state's highest point. This is Backbone Mountain. It stands 3,360 feet above sea level. North of Backbone is 6-square-mile Deep Creek Lake. This is the state's largest lake. It was formed by damming the Youghiogheny River. Other western rivers include the Monocacy, Patapsco, Patuxent, and Susquehanna.

WOODS, WILDLIFE, AND WEATHER

Maryland is four-tenths wooded. The white oak is the state tree. Maples, beeches, ashes, chestnuts,

The colors of the black-eyed Susan and Baltimore oriole are similar to those of the state flag.

Left: Wild ponies on Assateague Island Right: Autumn along the Youghiogheny River

pines, and hickories also grow there. The black-eyed Susan is the state flower.

The Baltimore oriole is the state bird. Bald eagles nest in Maryland. Black bears roam the mountains. Assateague Island is famous for its wild ponies. Diamondback terrapin turtles live along the coast. Their shells have diamond patterns. Oysters, shrimps, clams, and crabs are found in coastal waters. The striped bass, or rockfish, is the state fish. Maryland even has a state insect—the Baltimore checkerspot butterfly.

Maryland has a warm, wet climate. Summer temperatures often rise above 85 degrees Fahrenheit. On many winter days, the temperature tops 40 degrees Fahrenheit. But throughout the year, it is cooler in the western mountains. The far-western mountains receive about 7 feet of snow each year. Garrett County had 12.5 feet of snow in the winter of 1960-61. The Eastern Shore receives less than 1 foot of snow each winter.

Winter in Cunningham Falls State Park

From Ancient Times Until Today

From Ancient Times Until Today

Dinosaurs roamed across Maryland more than 100 million years ago. They included the allosaurus. In later times, Maryland was under water. Fossils of crocodiles and giant sharks have been found there.

Opposite: A replica of the Dove, *one of the two ships that brought English settlers to Maryland in 1634*

American Indians

The first people reached Maryland more than 10,000 years ago. These were prehistoric Indians. They hunted with stone-tipped spears.

By the 1600s, many Indian tribes lived in Maryland. Susquehannocks lived at Chesapeake Bay's northern end. Nanticokes, Choptanks, Pocomokes, and Wicomicos were on the Eastern Shore. Piscataways and Patuxents were on the Western Shore.

The Indians lived in villages. Their homes were called wigwams. These "longhouses" had rounded roofs. They were made of wood and tree bark. The Indians hunted bears and deer. They grew corn, beans, squash, and tobacco. Children helped by gathering clams, oysters, and berries.

An Indian longhouse at St. Mary's City

George Calvert

EUROPEAN EXPLORERS AND SETTLERS

Giovanni da Verrazano was an Italian explorer. He studied North America's Atlantic Coast for France. Verrazano may have sailed up Chesapeake Bay in 1524. Spanish sailors arrived soon after. Neither France nor Spain settled Maryland, though.

In 1607, England settled Virginia. That was the first of the thirteen colonies. John Smith, a Virginia leader, explored Maryland in 1608. He reached the spots where Washington, D.C., and Baltimore now stand.

In 1631, William Claiborne left Virginia. He began a trading post on Kent Island. That island is in Chesapeake Bay. His outpost was Maryland's first English settlement.

Meanwhile, George Calvert had decided to settle a colony in Maryland. Calvert is better known as Lord Baltimore. Calvert was a Roman Catholic. But he once had been a Protestant. He wanted people from all Christian faiths to live in his colony. In 1632, King Charles I gave Calvert all the land in present-day Maryland.

George Calvert died before starting his colony. His son, Cecil Calvert, became the second Lord Baltimore. Cecil sent the first 150 settlers to

Maryland. Their ships, the *Ark* and the *Dove*, reached Maryland in March 1634. Leonard Calvert, Cecil's younger brother, was governor of the new colony. Leonard made friends with the Indians. For some tools and cloth, he bought the Yaocomico Indians' village. The colonists then had a ready-made town. There were even wigwams for their first homes.

Governor Leonard Calvert named the town St. Mary's. Later, the name was changed to St. Mary's City. From 1634 to 1694, St. Mary's City was Maryland's capital.

Leonard Calvert and the English settlers landing at St. Mary's

COLONIAL TIMES

The Calverts controlled Maryland during most of
the colonial years. Maryland prospered under them.
Many people came there to grow tobacco. By the
1680s, Marylanders depended heavily on slaves to
grow this crop. Some huge farms called plantations
had dozens of slaves. Other Marylanders grew rich
by shipping goods to England or by making iron.

In 1649, Maryland's assembly passed the
Toleration Act. This gave religious freedom to all
Christians. Annapolis was begun in 1649 by
Puritans from Virginia. In 1694, Annapolis became
Maryland's capital. Maryland's first free school was
founded in Annapolis in 1696. Today, it is St.
John's College. In 1699, Thomas Bray set up thirty
libraries in Maryland. The *Maryland Gazette* was

Maryland's first newspaper. It was begun in Annapolis in 1727.

More towns were begun. Baltimore was founded in 1729. Soon pioneers moved into western Maryland. German people led the settlement of that area. Many of them came from Pennsylvania. Frederick and Hagerstown were begun by 1750. Maryland's population had reached 162,000 by 1760. Only three colonies had more people.

THE REVOLUTIONARY WAR

William Paca

By 1763, England's government was deeply in debt. To raise money, England decided to tax the American colonists. The colonists refused to pay the taxes. They also stopped buying English goods. In 1774, the ship *Peggy Stewart* reached Annapolis. It was carrying British tea. Marylanders forced the owner to burn the ship. This is called the *Peggy Stewart* Tea Party.

Samuel Chase

In 1776, the thirteen colonies broke from England. Through the Declaration of Independence, they became the United States. Four Marylanders signed this important paper. They were Samuel Chase, William Paca, Thomas Stone, and Charles Carroll of Carrollton.

The Treaty of Paris, which officially ended the Revolutionary War, was signed in this room in the Maryland State House in 1784.

To win its freedom, the United States fought England in the Revolutionary War. Maryland provided 23,000 troops. General George Washington praised Maryland's soldiers. He called them "troops of the line." Baltimore served as the country's capital (December 1776-March 1777) during part of the war. When the war ended, Annapolis was the country's capital (November 1783-June 1784). There, Washington resigned as head of the American army. Also in Annapolis, Congress signed the peace treaty that officially ended the war.

GROWTH OF MARYLAND

In the early years, the United States had a weak government. Each state made its own laws. In 1786, Annapolis hosted a meeting about trade problems among the states. The next year, a larger meeting was held in Philadelphia. There, America's leaders wrote the United States Constitution. It set up the country's framework of government. Three Maryland leaders signed the Constitution. They were James McHenry, Daniel Carroll, and Daniel of St. Thomas Jenifer. Maryland approved the Constitution on April 28, 1788. Maryland then became the seventh state.

The Constitution called for one place to be the country's permanent capital. In 1791, Maryland gave up land for the new United States capital. The capital was named Washington, D.C., in honor of President George Washington.

America and England went to war again in 1812. This War of 1812 lasted until 1815. Many ships built in Baltimore attacked English ships. In August 1814, the English attacked Washington, D.C. They burned the White House and the Capitol. They also hoped to destroy Baltimore's shipyards. In September 1814, English ships fired on Fort McHenry. The fort guarded Baltimore's harbor.

Marylander Francis Scott Key had been captured by the English. He watched the attack from a

The Francis Scott Key Memorial, Fort McHenry

The bombardment of Fort McHenry

Left: A canal boat on the Chesapeake and Ohio Canal
Right: Railroad cars at the Baltimore and Ohio Railroad Museum, in Baltimore

nearby boat. In the dawn's early light, Key saw a welcome sight. The United States flag still flew over the fort. Baltimore had not fallen to the enemy. Key wrote "The Star-Spangled Banner" to express his joy. Today, it is the national anthem.

In the early 1800s, Maryland grew rapidly. By 1810, Baltimore was the country's third-largest city. The young state also became a transportation center. The National Road was opened to the public in 1818. It led from Cumberland, Maryland, to Wheeling, in present-day West Virginia. In 1840, this 800-mile road stretched to Vandalia, Illinois. Thousands of families traveled west on this road.

Goods were shipped to the east and the west from Maryland on canals. In 1828, work started on the Chesapeake and Ohio Canal, but this canal was never completed. The Chesapeake and Delaware Canal opened in 1829. It linked cities on northern Chesapeake Bay with the Atlantic Ocean.

By 1830, the Baltimore and Ohio (B & O) Railroad had laid tracks across Maryland. Baltimore was also a shipbuilding center. The *Ann McKim* was launched from there in 1833. It was one of the world's fastest clipper ships. The *De Rosset* was built in Baltimore in 1839. It was the country's first oceangoing steamship made of iron.

SLAVERY AND THE CIVIL WAR

In the 1800s, the North and the South argued over slavery and other things. Many northerners felt the United States government should outlaw slavery in the South. Slavery had been outlawed in the North since the early 1800s. Southerners believed each state should decide for itself about slavery. Finally, eleven southern states left the Union. They formed the Confederate States of America. The North (Union) and the South (Confederacy) then fought the Civil War (1861-1865).

A canal is a man-made waterway that links two bodies of water. The Chesapeake and Ohio was designed to connect the bay to the Ohio River.

Clipper ships were small, fast sailing vessels.

Costumed actors reenact a Civil War battle

Maryland was thought of as a southern slave state. In 1860, more than 13,000 Marylanders still owned slaves. Yet the state had strong trading ties with the North. Maryland also had the largest number of free black people. Maryland decided to stay in the Union. But many Marylanders sided with the South. President Abraham Lincoln sent Union troops into Maryland. He wanted to make sure that Maryland remained in the Union. If it hadn't, Washington, D.C., would have been surrounded by Confederate states.

The Old Line State provided 50,000 Union troops. They included 10,000 free black men.

The Battle of Antietam

However, another 22,000 Marylanders marched off to serve the South. Many Maryland families had members in both armies.

Few battles took place in Maryland. One was the bloodiest one-day battle ever fought on American soil. On September 17, 1862, 41,000 Southern troops fought 87,000 Union troops. The Union won this Battle of Antietam near Sharpsburg. Nearly 11,000 men on each side were killed or wounded.

Few cities in the nation at that time had as many people as fought at Antietam.

In 1864, Maryland's government outlawed slavery. On April 9, 1865, the war ended. The Union had won. The country's remaining slaves were freed. On April 14, Marylander John Wilkes Booth shot President Lincoln. Lincoln died the next day.

John Wilkes Booth

Industry, Culture, Wars, and Depression

After the war, Maryland's industries continued to grow. Clothing, furniture, and foods were made in Baltimore and other cities. Thousands of Europeans came to live and work in Maryland. By 1910, the state's population was 1,295,346.

Baltimore was becoming a great city. Many rich bankers, merchants, and railroad owners lived there. Some of them gave their money for schools,

libraries, and hospitals. George Peabody set up the Peabody Institute in 1868. This became a great music school. It also has a large library. In 1882, Enoch Pratt began the Enoch Pratt Free Library. In 1876, Johns Hopkins University opened. Johns Hopkins Hospital opened in 1889. Both places were built with money left by Johns Hopkins.

In 1917, the United States entered World War I (1914-1918). That year the army opened Fort George G. Meade. More than 100,000 soldiers were trained there. Also in 1917, Maryland's Aberdeen Proving Ground was built. Weapons were tested there. More than 62,000 Maryland soldiers and 500 nurses helped win the war.

Most Marylanders enjoyed the good times of the 1920s. Then the Great Depression (1929-1939) hit the United States. By 1932, more than half of Maryland's factories had closed. Others were running only part-time. Governor Albert Ritchie led the state during those hard times.

World War II (1939-1945) helped end the Great Depression. The United States entered the war in 1941. About 250,000 Maryland men and women served. In 1942, Andrews Air Force Base opened. It was built to guard Washington, D.C. The state's factories made ships and airplanes.

These gas mortars were developed at an army center in Edgewood during World War II.

CHALLENGES OF CHANGE

In 1902, Maryland's government had taken away many rights of black people. The other southern states had done this also. Black students and white students had separate schools. Black people and white people also had to sit in separate parts of restaurants and buses. In 1954, the United States Supreme Court ordered an end to segregated

This man is rehabbing his old Baltimore row house in the city's redevelopment area. Baltimore is famous for its row houses. They are brick houses that are attached to one another.

SAVE THE BAY is a slogan on Maryland license plates.

schools. America's public schools had to admit both black students and white students. Baltimore quickly integrated its schools. Other Maryland cities followed. During the 1960s, Maryland stopped separating the races in public places.

Since 1950, Baltimore has lost about 200,000 people. Many white Baltimoreans moved to the suburbs. Today, about six out of ten Baltimoreans are black. Many are very poor. Baltimore has had a high jobless rate in recent years. Between 1970 and 1990, Baltimore lost more than 40,000 manufacturing jobs.

Baltimore is bouncing back, though. Since 1970, parts of Baltimore have been rebuilt. The Inner Harbor was completed in the 1980s. It features shops and restaurants. Baltimore's Seagirt Marine Terminal opened in 1990. Maryland-made machines and chemicals are sent around the world from this port. Baltimore's schools are also trying a new program. A private company runs some of its schools. The students' math and reading scores are rising. The program may become a model for other American schools.

Pollution in Chesapeake Bay is another problem. Pollution and over-harvesting have nearly destroyed the bay's oysters. The striped bass catch has dropped greatly. Since 1985, Marylanders have

worked to clean the bay. Industries and farmers are working to keep waste out of the bay.

⌐ Maryland reached a milestone in 1988. April 28 marked the state's 200th birthday. Marylanders are proud of their history. The Old Line State gave the country its capital and "The Star-Spangled Banner." Marylanders hope for a star-spangled future, too.

Baltimore's Inner Harbor

Overleaf: Two women in African dress take part in Baltimore's Annual Celebration of the Arts.

Marylanders and Their Work

MARYLANDERS AND THEIR WORK

There are about 4.8 million Marylanders. Almost one-half of them live in and around Baltimore. Another one-third live in Maryland's suburbs of Washington, D.C. The remaining one-sixth live in small towns or on farms widely spread over the rest of the state. Most Marylanders live well. Their average yearly income is $23,000.

Seven of every ten Marylanders are white. One-fourth of them are of German ancestry. Other white Marylanders have English, Polish, Italian, and Irish backgrounds.

One-fourth of all Marylanders are black. By 1990, about 140,000 Marylanders had Asian backgrounds. More than 125,000 Marylanders are Hispanic. They have Spanish-speaking backgrounds. Nearly 13,000 Native Americans live in the Old Line State.

A Korean Festival at Hopkins Plaza, Baltimore

These costumed children live in Baltimore's "Little Italy."

MARYLANDERS AT WORK

About 2.5 million Marylanders have jobs. Service work is the state's leading kind of job. There are

Electronic assembly at Aliant Technical Systems, Annapolis

Maryland raises 250 million broiler chickens a year—one for each American.

almost 600,000 service workers in Maryland. The state has a large number of doctors and lawyers. People who fix cars and computers are some other service workers. Hotels hire many service workers. Marriott International is based in Bethesda. This company runs more than 700 hotels in 20 countries.

About 500,000 Marylanders sell goods. Giant Food, Inc., is a grocery chain with more than 150 stores. It is based in Landover. Over 400,000 Marylanders do government work. Maryland has thousands of United States government workers. Many work at the United States Census Bureau in Suitland. Others are with the Goddard Space Flight Center.

Nearly 200,000 Marylanders make goods. Electric machinery is the state's leading product. Foods are other Maryland products. McCormick & Company is the world's top seller of spices. It is near Baltimore. Medical and scientific instruments are also made in Maryland. Other products include paints, chemicals, ships, and steel.

More than 130,000 Marylanders work in banking, real estate, and insurance. About 170,000 work in construction. Few states have more builders.

Maryland has about 40,000 farmers. Broiler chickens are the state's top farm product. Maryland

ranks high at growing tobacco and tomatoes. Eggs, soybeans, corn, wheat, and milk are other Maryland farm goods.

A few thousand people make Maryland a leader at catching seafood. Crabs, clams, oysters, and flounder are caught in Maryland waters. Steamed crabs and crab cakes are famous Maryland dishes.

These clammers are bringing in their catch.

Overleaf: The skyline of Baltimore

31

A Tour of the Old Line State

A TOUR OF THE OLD LINE STATE

Maryland has plenty to offer visitors. They can learn about important people and places in the state's history. Visitors also enjoy Maryland's cities and towns, seashore and mountains.

THE EASTERN SHORE

About 270,000 people live on Maryland's Eastern Shore. Baltimore alone has nearly three times as many people. The Eastern Shore is known for fishing and farming. It is also a vacationland.

A huge sand castle at Ocean City

The Eastern Shore has about 30 miles of Atlantic coastline. Ocean City lies along the coast. This resort town is a good place to sunbathe, swim, and sail. Many people go out from Ocean City for deep-sea fishing. A bridge leads south to Assateague Island from Ocean City. The island is famous for its wild ponies. Many shorebirds also live there.

On the mainland are the Pocomoke Cypress Swamps. They run from Pocomoke Sound to Delaware. The swamps can be explored by boat or on foot. Bald cypress trees grow there.

Ocean City beach

Winners of Crisfield's 1991 Little Mr. Crustacean and Miss Crustacean contest

Crisfield is on the Eastern Shore's southwestern tip. It is called the "Seafood Capital of the World." Many of its people catch and pack seafood. Crisfield's sightseeing boats take visitors to nearby islands in Chesapeake Bay. Salisbury is north of Crisfield. It is the Eastern Shore's largest city. About 21,000 people live there. River Walk Park winds along the Wicomico River in downtown Salisbury. Pemberton Hall is another Salisbury attraction. This beautiful plantation was built in 1741.

Cambridge is northwest of Salisbury. It is the seat of Dorchester County. The Dorchester County Historical Society is in Cambridge. Children enjoy the society's antique toys and dolls. South of

Canada geese and snow geese at Blackwater National Wildlife Refuge

The Chesapeake Bay Maritime Museum at St. Michaels

Cambridge is Blackwater National Wildlife Refuge. Canada geese, peregrine falcons, and Delmarva fox squirrels live there. Horsehead Wetlands Center is north of Cambridge. Deer, red foxes, and bald eagles can be spotted around these wetlands.

St. Michaels is northwest of Cambridge. The Chesapeake Bay Maritime Museum is there. This museum has twelve buildings, including a lighthouse. Boats such as the skipjack can also be seen there. The skipjack is the state boat. To the north is Wye Oak State Park. The Wye Oak stands there. It is the country's largest white oak. The tree is more

than 400 years old. It towers over 100 feet high. Its trunk is 374 inches around. The white oak was chosen as Maryland's state tree because of the Wye Oak.

Chestertown is farther north on the Eastern Shore. The Geddes-Piper House in Chestertown was begun around 1780. Its furnishings recreate a house of Revolutionary War times. Washington College in Chestertown dates from 1782. It was Maryland's first college. The college was named for George Washington.

A few miles north is Georgetown. The Kitty Knight House is there. During the War of 1812, the British burned Georgetown. Most of the townspeople fled. But Kitty Knight stayed. She protected her home and that of her next-door neighbor. The neighbor was too ill to move. The British tried to burn the houses. But Kitty beat the fire out with her broom. The British finally decided to spare the two homes. These were the only Georgetown houses not burned to the ground.

Chesapeake City is in the northern part of Maryland. The Chesapeake and Delaware Canal Museum is there. The museum shows how the canal was built in the 1820s. Ships still use the canal. They travel from Chesapeake Bay to Delaware Bay.

The Wye Oak

The Chesapeake and Delaware Canal is one of the world's busiest canals. Millions of tons of cargo pass through the canal each year.

Elkton is a few miles north of Chesapeake City. Near Elkton is Gilpin's Falls Bridge. It is a 119-foot-long covered bridge. The bridge is nearly 150 years old. Many other covered bridges are in this part of Maryland.

THE WESTERN SHORE

Havre de Grace is far north on the Western Shore. The town's French name means "harbor of grace." Havre de Grace's Concord Point Lighthouse dates from 1827. It was one of the longest-used lighthouses on the East Coast.

To the south is Baltimore. Begun in 1729, Baltimore is now Maryland's largest city. About 736,000 people live there. It is also the largest city in the fourteen southern states.

Baltimore has many places connected to "The Star-Spangled Banner." The Maryland Historical Society in Baltimore has Francis Scott Key's original poem. Mary Pickersgill sewed the flag in her home. Today, her home is open to visitors. It is called the Star-Spangled Banner Flag House. Fort McHenry, where the flag flew, also welcomes visitors.

Other Baltimore attractions are at Inner Harbor. The *Constellation* is docked there. This ship

Maryland has twenty-seven lighthouses.

Mary Pickersgill's flag is in the National Museum of American History in Washington, D.C.

was launched at Baltimore in 1797. It was the first United States Navy vessel to capture an enemy warship. Harborplace has buildings with dozens of shops and restaurants. Also within Inner Harbor is the World Trade Center. On its twenty-seventh floor is the Top of the World. From there, visitors can look out over Baltimore. A museum there tells about Baltimore's past. Inner Harbor also houses the Maryland Science Center and the National Aquarium. The Science Center is a good place to learn about the stars. Bottle-nosed dolphins and seals are among the aquarium's thousands of sea animals.

The frigate Constellation

Sea life at the National Aquarium

39

*Left: United States
Naval Academy
officers
Right: The Annapolis
Historic District*

Baltimore has many great museums. Artist Rembrandt Peale founded Baltimore's Peale Museum in 1814. Today, it is the country's oldest museum building. Displays on Baltimore history can be seen there. So can paintings by the Peale family. Baltimore has the country's first black-history wax museum. The Great Blacks in Wax Museum has more than 100 wax figures. More figures of famous black people are added each year.

Baltimore is also a great sports city. Babe Ruth was born in a Baltimore row house in 1895. Today, the Babe Ruth Birthplace has displays on this great home-run hitter. Baseball fans also come to

Baltimore to cheer the Orioles. The team was named for the state bird. The Orioles play at Camden Yards. The new ballpark was completed in 1992. Baltimore is home to Pimlico Race Course, too. Each May, the Preakness horse race is run there. The winning horse earns $500,000 and a blanket of black-eyed Susans.

The Baltimore Orioles play at Camden Yards.

Columbia is southwest of Baltimore. It is the state's third-largest city. The Maryland Museum of African Art is in Columbia. There, children can try on African masks. They can also play African drums and thumb pianos.

Annapolis is south of Baltimore. It lies where the Severn River empties into the Chesapeake Bay. Annapolis is known for its colonial buildings. Maryland lawmakers meet in the State House in Annapolis. It was begun in 1772. Now, it is the oldest capitol still used by a state legislature. It is also the only state house to have served as the United States Capitol (1783-1784).

Settled in 1649, Annapolis became Maryland's capital in 1694.

Horses racing in the Preakness

The United States Naval Academy opened in Annapolis in 1845. It still trains officers for the navy and marines. The academy also offers tours for visitors. The academy's museum is a good place to learn about naval history.

St. Mary's City is near the Western Shore's southern tip. An outdoor history museum is there.

Historic St. Mary's City

It is called Historic St. Mary's City. Part of Maryland's first English town has been rebuilt. Visitors can even board a replica of the *Dove*.

To the west are several large Maryland cities. They are close to Washington, D.C. Silver Spring has about 76,000 people. It is Maryland's second-largest city. The National Oceanic and Atmospheric Administration's (NOAA) main office is in Silver Spring. Part of NOAA's job is to forecast the weather. Bethesda is also outside Washington, D.C. With nearly 63,000 people, Bethesda is Maryland's fifth-biggest city. The National Institutes of Health (NIH) is in Bethesda. Scientists there do medical studies. Visitors can learn how they work to fight cancer, AIDS, and aging.

The Clara Barton National Historic Site is outside Bethesda. In 1881, Barton founded the American Red Cross. She was the Red Cross's first president. Her thirty-six-room home was Red Cross headquarters.

CENTRAL AND WESTERN MARYLAND

Rockville is just north of Bethesda. The Beall-Dawson House is a Rockville landmark. Built in 1815, it was Rockville's first brick house.

Frederick is northwest of Rockville. In 1862, southern troops marched through Frederick. They ordered the townspeople to lower the United States flag. Ninety-year-old Barbara Fritchie is said to have refused to do so. The Barbara Fritchie House and Museum in Frederick is her rebuilt home. Visitors can see clothes and quilts that Fritchie made.

Antietam Creek is west of Frederick. The Battle of Antietam was fought there in 1862. The site is now Antietam National Battlefield. One of its monuments is to Clara Barton. She was called the "Angel of the Battlefield." Barton brought medical supplies to the wounded during the fighting.

The Sunken Road, Antietam National Battlefield

Catoctin Mountain is north of Frederick. Camp David is there. For over fifty years, presidents have gone there to rest and to think. West of Catoctin Mountain is Hagerstown. It is in the Appalachian Valley. In 1737, Jonathan Hager settled there. Hagerstown is Maryland's biggest city west of Frederick. Over 35,000 people live there. Jonathan Hager's house is open to visitors. This stone house has furniture from the 1700s.

West of Hagerstown is Hancock. There, Maryland is at its narrowest. The state is just 2 miles wide from north to south. This land is called Maryland's "wasp waist."

Cumberland is west of Hancock. The town began as Fort Cumberland in the 1750s. George Washington commanded the fort. Today, visitors can see Washington's headquarters. It is the only part of Fort Cumberland that is still standing. The Western Maryland Scenic Railroad starts its trip at Cumberland. The train goes west through valleys and mountains. The trip covers the 16 miles to Frostburg. Then the train returns to Cumberland.

Garrett County is in westernmost Maryland. The county has few people but much beautiful scenery. People camp in its mountains. They fish and boat in its rivers and lakes. The Savage River

and Reservoir has a 5.5-mile white-water run. The Whitewater Canoe and Kayak World Championships were held there in 1989.

Huge boulders in Catoctin Mountain National Park

Oakland is in a beautiful part of far-western Maryland. Muddy Creek Falls is near Oakland. This waterfall has a 52-foot drop. To the north is the Cove. This is a good place to end a Maryland trip. The overlook from the Cove offers a great view of the valley below. Visitors can see distant mountains that reach into Pennsylvania.

A Gallery of Famous Marylanders

A GALLERY OF FAMOUS MARYLANDERS

There have been many famous Marylanders. They include political leaders, authors, and baseball stars.

Margaret Brent (1601-1671) was born in England. In 1639, she moved to St. Mary's City. There, she became the first Maryland woman to own land. Brent was placed in charge of Leonard Calvert's legal matters. This made her America's first woman lawyer as well. She asked for the right to vote. The assembly turned her down. Brent has been called "America's First Feminist."

Thomas Cresap (1694-1790) was also born in England. He moved to Maryland about 1717 and bought land. In the 1700s, Maryland and Pennsylvania had a border war. Cresap fought fiercely. Pennsylvanians called him the "Maryland Monster." Cresap's land is now in Pennsylvania. In 1741, he founded Oldtown. That is near Cumberland. George Washington visited Cresap in 1748. Cresap told him many woodland stories.

Benjamin Banneker (1731-1806) was born near Ellicott City. He was a free-born black man. Banneker became a clock-builder and an

Opposite: United States Supreme Court Justice Thurgood Marshall with his grandson

Benjamin Banneker

astronomer. His most famous work was as a surveyor. In 1791, he helped lay out plans for Washington, D.C.

Elizabeth Ann Seton (1774-1821) lived in Maryland for more than ten years. She opened a Catholic school in Baltimore in 1809. This began the country's Catholic school system. She also began the Sisters of Charity in Maryland. It was the first Catholic religious order founded in the United States. In 1975, she was named a saint by the Roman Catholic church.

Francis Scott Key (1779-1843) was born in Frederick County. He graduated from St. John's

College in Annapolis. Besides writing "The Star-Spangled Banner," Key was also a famous lawyer. He served as U.S. attorney for Washington, D.C. (1833-1841).

Frederick Douglass (1817-1895) was born a slave in Tuckahoe. **Harriet Tubman** (1820?-1913) was born a slave in Dorchester County. Both escaped from slavery. Douglass traveled through the North. He spoke and wrote against slavery. In New York, Douglass began the *North Star*. It was an anti-slavery newspaper. Tubman returned to the South nineteen times. She led more than 300 slaves to freedom in the North. Southerners offered $40,000 for her capture. But she never was caught.

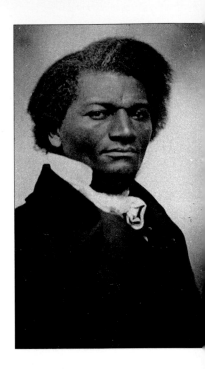

Frederick Douglass

Two famous brothers were born at a farm near Bel Air. **Edwin Booth** (1833-1893) became a world famous stage actor. **John Wilkes Booth** (1838-1865) was an actor, too. But he is remembered as the person who killed President Abraham Lincoln. Booth died a few days later.

Edwin Booth

Roger Taney (1777-1864) and **Thurgood Marshall** (1908-1993) served on the U.S. Supreme Court. Taney was born in Calvert County. He married Anne Key, Francis Scott Key's sister. Taney was chief justice of the Supreme Court (1836-1864). Marshall was born in Baltimore. He helped win the

Edgar Allan Poe

Helen Taussig

1954 case that integrated the country's schools. Marshall became the first black Supreme Court justice (1967-1991). He spoke for the poor.

Many great authors have been Marylanders. **Edgar Allan Poe** (1809-1849) was a master of scary tales. He lived in Baltimore when he first started writing. He died there during a later visit. "The Fall of the House of Usher" was one of his stories. **Upton Sinclair** (1878-1968) was born in Baltimore. He wrote novels that told how workers were mistreated. His novel *The Jungle* is about the meat-packing business. Poet **Adrienne Rich** was born in 1929 in Baltimore. Rich's *Diving into the Wreck* won the National Book Award (1974). **John Barth** was born in Cambridge in 1930. He writes novels that are like myths. *The Sot-Weed Factor* is one of them. **Anne Tyler** was born in 1941. She has lived in Baltimore since the 1960s. Many of her stories are set in that city. Tyler's book *The Accidental Tourist* was made into a movie. *Tumble Tower* (1993) is her first children's book. **Eubie Blake** (1883-1983) was born in Baltimore. He became a composer and pianist. "I'm Just Wild About Harry" is a famous Eubie Blake song. **Billie Holiday** (1915-1959) was also born in Baltimore. She became a famous jazz and blues singer. Holiday was known as

"Lady Day." The movie *Lady Sings the Blues* is about her life.

Matthew Henson (1866-1955) was born in Charles County. In 1888, he met explorer Robert Peary. In 1909, Henson was part of the first group to reach the North Pole. In 1912, Henson wrote about that trip. His book is called *A Negro Explorer at the North Pole.*

Dr. Helen Taussig (1898-1986) was born in Massachusetts. She became a children's doctor. Taussig headed Johns Hopkins Hospital's Children's Heart Clinic (1930-1963). There she helped develop the "blue-baby" operation. It has saved the lives of thousands of babies with heart

*Left: Billie Holiday
Right: Matthew Henson*

defects. Her work also led to modern open-heart surgery.

William Donald Schaefer was born in Baltimore in 1921. He has lived in the same Baltimore row house all his life. Schaefer was Baltimore's mayor from 1971 to 1986. No other Baltimore mayor served as long. He worked to build Inner Harbor and Harborplace. In 1986, he was elected Maryland's governor. He was reelected in 1990.

Kurt Schmoke was born in Baltimore in 1949. He followed Schaefer as Baltimore's mayor. Schmoke became Baltimore's first elected black mayor. He wants Baltimore to be "The City That Reads."

Barbara Mikulski was born in 1936 in Baltimore. She became a social worker, then a lawmaker. She served in the U.S. House of Representatives (1977-1987). In 1987, she became the first woman U.S. senator from Maryland.

Besides Babe Ruth, many other great baseball players have come from Maryland. **William "Judy" Johnson** (1899-1989) was born in Snow Hill. He was a great hitter in the Negro Leagues. Johnson played baseball before the major leagues admitted black players. **Al Kaline** was born in Baltimore in

Kurt Schmoke

Al Kaline (second from left) had more than 3,000 hits for the Detroit Tigers. He entered the Baseball Hall of Fame in 1980.

1934. He played right field for the Detroit Tigers. He is one of a few players with more than 3,000 hits. Kaline entered the Baseball Hall of Fame in 1980. **Cal Ripken, Jr.,** was born in Havre de Grace in 1960. This star shortstop for the Baltimore Orioles played in more than 1,000 consecutive games.

Birthplace of Babe Ruth, Benjamin Banneker, Harriet Tubman, and Barbara Mikulski . . .

Home, too, of Margaret Brent, Thomas Cresap, Dr. Helen Taussig, and Edgar Allan Poe . . .

Site of the U.S. Naval Academy, Camp David, and Clara Barton's home . . .

The place where the Battle of Antietam was fought and "The Star-Spangled Banner" was written . . .

This is Maryland—the Old Line State!

Did You Know?

The nation's motto, *In God We Trust,* appears on U.S. coins and paper money. The motto is thought to have come from verse four of "The Star-Spangled Banner." In it are the words: "And this be our motto: In God is our trust."

In 1904, Hagerstown librarian Mary Lemist Titcomb invented the bookmobile. Horses pulled that first library on wheels. The library's janitor drove the bookmobile over a 500-square-mile area.

Author Upton Sinclair entered college when he was fourteen. He wrote comics and adventure stories to pay his tuition. Sinclair produced 5,000 pages a year, including a 250-page novel that he wrote in less than a week.

In 1989, Jim Youngblood set a boomerang-throwing record at Gaithersburg. He threw a boomerang that traveled 440 feet and then returned to him.

The *Tom Thumb,* a steam locomotive, ran a two-part race against a horse-drawn railroad car in 1830. The locomotive won the 13-mile race from Baltimore to Ellicott City. But the horse won the return race to Baltimore. A drive belt broke on the *Tom Thumb.*

Charlie King was among the dead at the Battle of Antietam. The twelve-year-old drummer boy from Pennsylvania was the youngest soldier killed in the Civil War.

Maryland has towns named Accident, Loveville, Parole, and Friendly.

Maryland's Eastern Shore is on the Delmarva Peninsula. The name *Delmarva* was coined because the peninsula includes *Del*aware and parts of *Mar*yland and *Virginia*.

Ladiesburg is near Frederick. The town supposedly received its name because there were seven women for each man.

In the 1980s, young Colin McEwen found a fossil in Largo. It came from a plesiosaur. This was a long-necked sea creature that lived 100 million years ago.

Jousting is Maryland's state sport. Riders on horseback carrying poles called lances try to spear dangling rings. Towns in southern Maryland host the state jousting championships each fall. During the Middle Ages in Europe, jousting knights tried to knock one another off their horses with lances.

In 1990, eleven-year-old Richard Daff, Jr., of Crownsville became the youngest person to bowl a perfect 300 game.

"Your name is mud" is sometimes said to people who have caused trouble. Samuel Mudd, a Maryland doctor, set John Wilkes Booth's broken leg after Booth shot Abraham Lincoln. Dr. Mudd may not have known of the shooting. But for helping Booth, he was imprisoned. His name came to be an insult.

55

MARYLAND INFORMATION

State flag

Black-eyed Susans

Baltimore oriole

Area: 10,460 square miles (only eight states are smaller)

Greatest Distance North to South: 124 miles

Greatest Distance East to West: 238 miles

Borders: Pennsylvania to the north; Virginia, West Virginia, and Washington, D.C., along the south and west; Delaware and the Atlantic Ocean to the east

Highest Point: Backbone Mountain, 3,360 feet above sea level

Lowest Point: Sea level, along the Atlantic Ocean and Chesapeake Bay

Hottest Recorded Temperature: 109° F. (near Cumberland, on July 3, 1898; and at Cumberland and Frederick, on July 10, 1936)

Coldest Recorded Temperature: -40° F. (at Oakland, on January 13, 1912)

Statehood: The seventh state, on April 28, 1788

Origin of Name: King Charles I named the area Terra Maria (Latin, meaning "land of Maria") for his wife, Queen Henrietta Maria. In English, it became Maryland.

Capital: Annapolis

Counties: 23

United States Representatives: 8 (as of 1992)

State Senators: 47

State Delegates: 141

State Song: "Maryland, My Maryland," words by James R. Randall, sung to the tune of "O, Tannenbaum"

State Motto: *Fatti Maschii, Parole Femine* (Italian motto of the Calverts, meaning "manly deeds, gentle words")

Nicknames: "Old Line State," "Free State"

State Seal: Adopted in 1876   **State Flag:** Adopted in 1904

State Flower: Black-eyed Susan **State Tree:** White oak

State Bird: Baltimore oriole **State Fish:** Striped bass

State Dog: Chesapeake Bay retriever **State Sport:** Jousting

State Crustacean: Maryland blue crab **State Boat:** Skipjack

State Insect: Baltimore checkerspot butterfly

State Fossil Shell: *Ecphora quadricostata*

Some Rivers: Pocomoke, Wicomico, Nanticoke, Choptank, Chester, Susquehanna, Patapsco, Patuxent, Monocacy, Antietam Creek, Potomac

Wildlife: Deer, foxes, skunks, otters, black bears, squirrels, rabbits, chipmunks, wild ponies, Baltimore orioles, bald eagles, wild turkeys, geese, ducks, mockingbirds, other kinds of birds, diamondback terrapins, rattlesnakes, striped bass, sea trout, crabs, clams, oysters, many other water creatures

Manufactured Products: Soft drinks, spices, bread, other packaged foods, medical and scientific instruments, clothing, paints, chemicals, ships, steel, newspapers and other printed materials, roofing and paving materials, television equipment, other electrical communication goods

Farm Products: Broiler chickens, milk, beef cattle, hogs, eggs, tobacco, soybeans, corn, wheat, barley, hay, apples, tomatoes, flowers, shrubs, fruit trees

Mining Products: Crushed stone, coal, sand and gravel, natural gas, clay, limestone

Fishing Products: Crabs, clams, oysters, flounder, tuna, striped bass, bluefish, perch, catfish, menhaden

Population: 4,781,468, nineteenth among the fifty states (1990 U.S. Census Bureau figures)

Major Cities (1990 Census):

Baltimore	736,014	Wheaton	53,720
Silver Spring	76,046	Towson	49,445
Columbia	75,883	Potomac	45,634
Dundalk	65,800	Aspen Hill	45,494
Bethesda	62,936	Rockville	44,835

White oak

Blue crabs

Skipjack

MARYLAND HISTORY

St. John's College, in Annapolis, was founded in 1696.

8000 B.C.—Prehistoric Indians reach Maryland

1524—Giovanni da Verrazano explores along the Maryland coast

1608—Captain John Smith explores Maryland

1631—William Claiborne begins Maryland's first English settlement on Kent Island

1632—King Charles I of England grants Maryland to George Calvert, Lord Baltimore

1634—English colonists arrive and settle St. Mary's City

1649—Maryland's assembly passes the Toleration Act

1694—Annapolis becomes Maryland's capital

1696—Maryland's first free school (now St. John's College) is founded in Annapolis

1727—The colony's first newspaper, the *Maryland Gazette,* is published

1729—Baltimore is founded

1775—Revolutionary War begins

1776—American leaders issue the Declaration of Independence; Maryland adopts its first state constitution

1776-77—Baltimore is the U.S. capital, December to March

1781—Marylanders help win the Revolutionary War's last battle at Yorktown, Virginia

1783-84—Annapolis is the U.S. capital, November to June

1788—Maryland ratifies the U.S. Constitution and becomes the seventh state on April 28

1791—Maryland gives up land for Washington, D.C.

1800—Washington, D.C., becomes the permanent U.S. capital

1812-15—The United States fights the War of 1812 against England; warships are built in Baltimore

1814—Francis Scott Key writes "The Star-Spangled Banner"

1830—The B & O Railroad begins service

1844—The country's first telegraph line links Baltimore and Washington, D.C.

1845—The U.S. Naval Academy opens at Annapolis

1861—The Civil War begins; Maryland stays in the Union

1864—Maryland adopts a new constitution that forbids slavery

1865—The Union wins the Civil War and the country's remaining slaves are freed

1867—Maryland's present state constitution is adopted

1876—Baltimore's Johns Hopkins University opens

1889—Baltimore's Johns Hopkins Hospital opens

1917-18—Nearly 63,000 Marylanders serve in World War I

1929-39—The Great Depression brings hard times

1941-45—About 250,000 Marylanders help win World War II

1942—Andrews Air Force Base opens

1954—Baltimore lawyer Thurgood Marshall wins the Supreme Court case to integrate public schools

1967—Thurgood Marshall becomes the nation's first black U.S. Supreme Court judge

1970—The Baltimore Orioles win the World Series

1971—Parren Mitchell becomes the first black Marylander in the U.S. Congress; the Baltimore Colts win the Super Bowl

1981—The National Aquarium opens in Inner Harbor

1983—The Baltimore Orioles win the World Series

1987—Barbara Mikulski becomes Maryland's first woman in the U.S. Senate; Kurt Schmoke becomes Baltimore's first elected black mayor

1988—Happy 200th birthday, Old Line State!

1990—The state's population is 4,781,468; Baltimore's Seagirt Marine Terminal opens

1994—Annapolis celebrates 300 years as Maryland's capital

Barbara Mikulski (on the left) in 1987 became Maryland's first woman in the U. S. Senate.

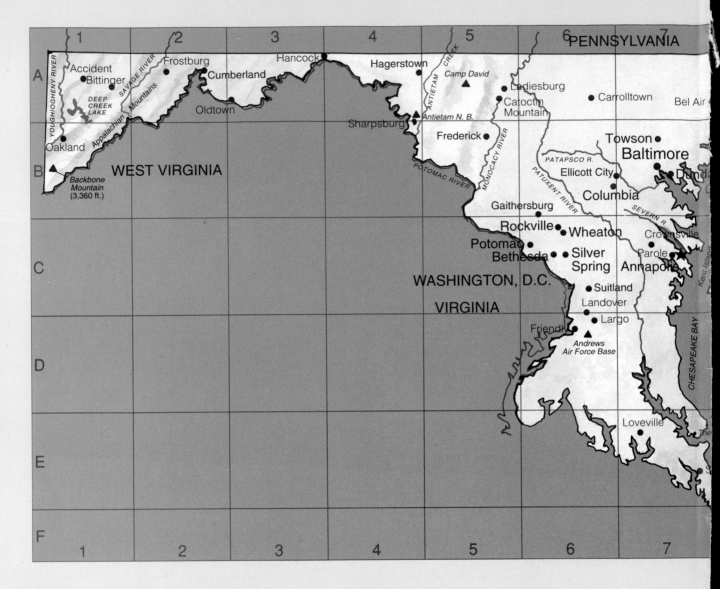

MAP KEY

GLOSSARY

ancient: Relating to a time long ago

antislavery: Against slavery

capital: The city that is the seat of government

capitol: The building in which the government meets

climate: A region's typical weather

clipper ship: A small, fast sailing vessel

coast: The land along a large body of water

colony: A settlement outside a parent country that is ruled by the parent country

constitution: A framework of government

explorer: A person who visits and studies unknown lands

feminist: Someone who works for women's rights

independence: Being free from another's control

industry: Business activity

integrate: To bring people of various races together

61

legislature: A lawmaking body

manufacturing: The making of products

national anthem: A country's official song

permanent: Lasting

plantation: A very large farm

pollution: The harming of the environment

population: The number of people in a place

prehistoric: Belonging to the time before written history

slavery: A practice in which some people are owned by other people

swamp: A wetland

surveyor: Someone who figures land boundaries

PICTURE ACKNOWLEDGMENTS

Front cover, © Dan Beigel Photography/**N E Stock Photo;** 1, © **Cameramann International, Ltd.;** 2, **Tom Dunnington;** 3, © **Kevin Fleming;** 4-5, **Tom Dunnington;** 6-7, © Eugene L. Drifmeyer/**Photri;** 8, © Brent Parrett/**N E Stock Photo;** 9, **Courtesy of Hammond, Incorporated, Maplewood, New Jersey;** 10 (left), © **Kevin Fleming;** 10 (right), © Larry Ulrich/**Tony Stone Images, Inc.;** 11, © **Tom Dietrich;** 12, © **Joan Dunlop;** 13, © Bill Howe/**Photri;** 14, **North Wind Picture Archives;** 15, **Maryland Historical Society, Baltimore;** 16, **Maryland Historical Society, Baltimore** (detail); 17 (both pictures), **Maryland Historical Society, Baltimore;** 18, © Doris De Witt/**Tony Stone Images, Inc.;** 19 (top), © Mick Roessler/**SuperStock;** 19 (bottom), **Maryland Historical Society, Baltimore;** 20 (left), © **Tom Dietrich;** 20 (right), © Everett C. Johnson/**mga/Photri;** 21, **Maryland Office of Tourism Development, photo by Middleton Evans;** 22, **Stock Montage, Inc.;** 23, **Stock Montage, Inc.;** 24, **Stock Montage, Inc.;** 25, **AP/Wide World Photos;** 26, © **Cameramann International, Ltd.;** 27, © Bill Howe/**Photri;** 28, © **Middleton Evans;** 29 (both pictures), © **Middleton Evans;** 30, © **Dan Beigel Photography/N E Stock Photo;** 31, © E. Drifmeyer/**Photri;** 32-33, © **Tom Till;** 34, © **Middleton Evans;** 35 (both pictures), © **Kevin Fleming;** 36 (top), © Christian Titlow/**Photri;** 36 (bottom), © Everett C. Johnson/**mga/Photri;** 37, © **Kevin Fleming;** 39 (top), © Michael Ma Po Shum/**Tony Stone Images, Inc.;** 39 (bottom), © **Mae Scanlan;** 40 (both pictures), © **Kevin Fleming;** 41 (both pictures), **Maryland Office of Tourism Development, photo by Middleton Evans;** 42, © **Photri;** 43, © **Tom Till;** 44, © **Tom Dietrich;** 45, © **Tom Till;** 46, **AP/Wide World Photos;** 47, **Stock Montage, Inc.;** 48 (left), **National Park Service;** 48 (right), **Maryland Historical Society, Baltimore;** 49 (top), **AP/Wide World Photos;** 49 (bottom), **Stock Montage, Inc.;** 50 (top), **North Wind Picture Archives;** 50 (bottom), **AP/Wide World Photos;** 51 (left), **AP/Wide World Photos;** 51 (right), **Stock Montage, Inc.;** 52, **AP/Wide World Photos;** 53, **AP/Wide World Photos;** 54 (top), **Minnesota Historical Society;** 54-55 (bottom), **Maryland Historical Society, Baltimore;** 55 (top), © **Photri;** 56 (top), **Courtesy Flag Research Center, Winchester, Massachusetts 01890;** 56 (middle), © Ellsworth/**Photri;** 56 (bottom), © Rob Simpson/**Photri;** 57 (top), © **Jerry Hennen;** 57 (middle), © Bill Howe/**Photri;** 57 (bottom), © **Dan Beigel Photography/NE Stock Photo;** 58, © Bill Howe/**Photri;** 59, **AP/Wide world Photos;** 60-61, **Tom Dunnington;** back cover, © **Mae Scanlan**

INDEX

Page numbers in boldface type indicate illustrations.

ABOUT THE AUTHOR

Dennis Brindell Fradin is the author of 150 published children's books. His works for Childrens Press include the Young People's Stories of Our States series, the Disaster! series, and the Thirteen Colonies series. Dennis is married to Judith Bloom Fradin, who taught high-school and college English for many years. She is now Dennis's chief researcher. The Fradins are the parents of two sons, Anthony and Michael, and a daughter, Diana. Dennis graduated from Northwestern University in 1967 with a B.A. in creative writing, and has lived in Evanston, Illinois, since that year.